Our Camping Trip

by Ruth Welch

Contents

Going camping	2
Putting up the tent	4
In the afternoon	6
Cooking dinner	8
Going to sleep	10
Index	Inside back cover

Going Camping

We went camping with my dad.
I helped Dad to pack the car.

My sister helped too.

We took these things:

Putting up the tent

We found a good place to camp.
I helped Dad to put up the tent.

My sister helped too.

We used these things:

In the afternoon

We played outside.

Dad and I played with the kite.

My sister played too.

We used these things:

Cooking dinner

We cooked dinner outside.

I helped Dad to cook our food.

My sister helped too.

We used these things:

Going to sleep

We went to bed in our sleeping bags. I helped Dad to put them out.

My sister helped too.

We used these things:

Our camping trip was fun!